TOP DOG Breeds

FRENCH BULLDOGS

Christina Earley

Table of Contents

A Starfish Book

SEAHORSE PUBLISHING

Teaching Tips for Caregivers:

As a caregiver, you can help your child succeed in school by giving them a strong foundation in language and literacy skills and a desire to learn to read.

This book helps children grow by letting them practice reading skills.

Reading for pleasure and interest will help your child develop reading skills and will give your child the opportunity to practice these skills in meaningful ways.

- Encourage your child to read on their own at home.
- Encourage your child to practice reading aloud.
- Encourage activities that require reading.
- Establish a reading time.
- Talk with your child.
- Give your child writing materials.

Teaching Tips for Teachers:

Research shows that one of the best ways for students to learn a new topic is to read about it.

Before Reading

- Read the "Words to Know" and discuss the meaning of each word.
- Read the back cover to see what the book is about.

During Reading

- When a student gets to a word that is unknown, ask them to look at the rest of the sentence to find clues to help with the meaning of the unknown word.
- Ask the student to write down any pages of the book that were confusing to them.

After Reading

- Discuss the main idea of the book.
- Ask students to give one detail that they learned from the book by showing a text-dependent answer from the book.

French Bulldogs

Woof! Woof!

French bulldogs are **popular** pets.

French bulldogs are small-sized dogs. They have flat faces with **wrinkles**.

Fun Fact

Some French bulldog colors are fawn, white, and brindle.

French bulldogs are non-sporting dogs.

They are good family and house dogs.

A French bulldog's **coat** is short and smooth.

These dogs walk with a bowlegged **gait**.

French bulldogs enjoy sleeping.

They also love to play.

French bulldogs are smart.

They like to learn new tricks.

Fun Fact

Most French bulldogs can't swim.

French bulldogs need to eat two meals each day.

They need to be brushed one time each month.

French bulldogs bark only when there is a good reason.

These dogs make good **watchdogs**!

Fun Fact

French bulldogs are very sensitive to scolding.

The singer Lady Gaga owns three French bulldogs.

Actor Dwyane Johnson also has a French bulldog.

Quiz: Am I Ready for a Dog?

Find out if you are ready to own a dog.

Answer *yes* or *no* for each question.

1. I will help with feeding.
2. I will scoop poop.
3. I will help with training.
4. I will help with exercise.
5. I will be okay if some of my things get ruined.

Scoring:

Give yourself one point for each *yes* answer. Then, count up your total.

4 to 5: You are ready to talk to your caregivers about getting a dog.

2 to 3: You are not quite ready yet. Maybe next year.

0 to 1: You are not ready at all.

Staying Safe Around Dogs

DO	DO NOT
✓ Ask permission to pet a dog.	✗ Run up to a dog.
✓ Let the dog sniff your closed hand before petting.	✗ Bark or growl at a dog.
✓ Leave a dog alone when it is eating and sleeping.	✗ Ride or sit on a dog.
✓ Notice and listen to a dog's body language.	✗ Pull a dog's ears or tail.
✓ Respect a dog's space.	✗ Tease a dog.

Words to Know

coat (koht): the hair that covers a dog

gait (gayt): way of walking

popular (PAHP-yuh-lur): liked by many

watchdogs (WAHCH-dawgs): dogs kept to guard property

wrinkles (RING-kuhlz): lines and creases in skin

Index

Comprehension Questions

1. French bulldogs are ______ dogs.
   a. sporting
   b. herding
   c. non-sporting
2. A French bulldog's coat is _____.
   a. short b. doubled c. rough
3. How many times should you feed a French bulldog each day?
   a. once b. three times c. twice
4. **True or False:** French bulldogs are good watchdogs.
5. **True or False:** French bulldogs like to learn new tricks.

Answers
1. c 2. a 3. c 4. True 5. True

About the Author

Christina Earley lives in south Florida with her husband, son, and dog Bailey. When she is not writing books, she visits her local Humane Society to play with the dogs, cats, and bunnies. She likes to hike in the mountains and bake chocolate chip cookies.

Written by: Christina Earley
Design by: Kathy Walsh
Editor: Kim Thompson

Library of Congress PCN Data
French Bulldogs / Christina Earley
Top Dog Breeds
ISBN 979-8-8873-5946-5 (hard cover)
ISBN 979-8-8873-5985-4 (paperback)
ISBN 979-8-8904-2044-2 (EPUB)
ISBN 979-8-8904-2103-6 (eBook)
Library of Congress Control Number: 2023912469

Printed in the United States of America.

Photographs/Shutterstock: Cover & Title pg: grafienver_icons_logo, Ivanna-Ivashka, pnDl, provector, higedanddy, Nynke van Holten; pg numbers: Alemon cz; Fun Facts p 4, 13, 17: Elena Pimukova; p 21: Chief Design; p 3, 5, 7, 9, 11, 13, 15, 17, 19 Ivanna_Ivashka; p 3: mala_koza; p 4: Grisha Bruev; p 5: Csanad Kiss; p 6: tigercay_lpg; p 7: Southworks; p 8: Happy monkey; p 9: Eve Photography; p 10: Super_T; p 11: OlgaOvcharenko; p 12: Irina Kozorog; p 13: immstudio; p 14: Africa Studio; p 15: hedgehog94; p 16: Penyushkina; p 17: Irina Kozorog; p 18: Andrea Raffin; p 19: Mark Fann; P 21: Manop Boonpeng

Seahorse Publishing Company
www.seahorsepub.com

Published in the United States
Seahorse Publishing
PO Box 771325
Coral Springs, FL 33077

SEAHORSE PUBLISHING